CONTENTS

Look! That spider is missing a leg! But don't worry, it will grow back. Some animals can regrow their limbs, organs and skin. This is called regeneration. Many animals lose body parts while escaping from predators. A lost limb distracts the predator and gives the animal a chance to get away.

It's STILL ALIVE!

Magical Animals That Regrow Parts

by Nikki Potts

A+
books

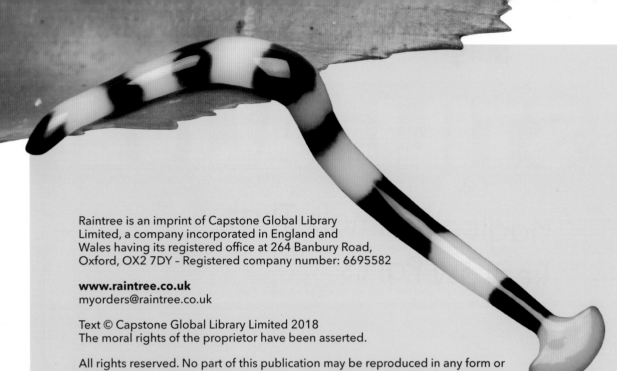

Raintree is an imprint of Capstone Global Library
Limited, a company incorporated in England and
Wales having its registered office at 264 Banbury Road,
Oxford, OX2 7DY – Registered company number: 6695582

www.raintree.co.uk
myorders@raintree.co.uk

Edited by Jaclyn Jaycox
Designed by Ashlee Suker
Picture research by Tracy Cummins
Production by Tori Abraham
Originated by Capstone Global Library Ltd
Printed and bound in India

ISBN 978 1 4747 5161 2 (hardback)
21 20 19 18 17
10 9 8 7 6 5 4 3 2 1

ISBN 978 1 4747 5165 0 (paperback)
22 21 20 19
10 9 8 7 6 5 4 3 2 1

British Library Cataloguing in Publication Data
A full catalogue record for this book is available from the British Library.

Acknowledgements
We would like to thank the following for permission to reproduce photographs: Alamy: Shay Levy, 16;
iStockphoto: somethingway, 28, wblom, 11; Minden Pictures: Alex Mustard, 15, Sue Daly, 9; Newscom: W.
Layer/picture alliance/blickwinkel, 17; Science Source: Dr. Keith Wheeler, 21, Eye of Science, 27, James H.
Robinson, 13, Tom McHugh, 22; Shutterstock: 3Dstock, 26, Adam Kel, 8, Cigdem Sean Cooper, 29, Decha
Thapanya, 4-5, dossyl, Cover Back, 12, Ethan Daniels, 19, George P Gross, 14, Kazakov Maksim, 24, kurt_G
Stock, Cover, Matt Jeppson, 23, Najmie Naharuddin, 2, 20, reptiles4all, 1, Rich Carey, 18, Robert F Apple, 10,
Sergio Gutierrez Getino, 6, topimages, 25, Victor Saul, 7

MEXICAN AXOLOTL

Mexican axolotls are found in waters near Mexico City. Unlike many amphibians, axolotls keep their gills into adulthood. Axolotls can be up to 30 centimetres (12 inches) long. Most axolotls live for up to 15 years. They are able to regenerate many body parts. Limbs, jaws, tails, skin and spinal cords can all be regrown.

:: **FUN FACT** ::

Axolotls can be black, brown, white or albino. Mexican axolotls are an endangered species.

STARFISH

Despite their name, starfish are not actually fish. Starfish live in deep or shallow ocean water. There are 2,000 species of starfish. The largest can weigh nearly 5 kilograms (11 pounds). Most starfish have 5 arms, but some species have up to 40 arms! A starfish's arms often contain its most important organs. Many species can regrow arms. Some starfish can regrow a whole new body from just part of one arm.

A starfish has no brain
and no blood.

SPIDER

Spiders are found on every continent except Antarctica. Plenty of predators hunt for spiders. A predator may damage a spider's leg by biting it. The spider then often detaches its leg for defence. This is called autotomy. Losing a leg may save a spider's life. The leg will grow back in time.

missing legs

:: FUN FACT ::

Spiders are arachnids. Insects have six legs and three body sections. Arachnids have only two body sections and eight legs.

ANOLE LIZARD

Anole lizards are also masters of autotomy. This lizard contracts muscles in order to cut off its tail. The detached tail distracts predators. Later, a new tail grows in its place. The new tail is made of cartilage instead of bones. Anole lizards are found throughout the southern United States. Most do not live for more than three years in the wild.

:: **FUN FACT** ::

A queen conch can live
for 20 to 30 years.

CONCH

Conches are saltwater snails. A conch has a spiral shell with short spikes sticking out. An adult's shell can be 15 to 30 centimetres (6 to 12 inches) long. A conch has excellent vision. This snail is able to pull its eyes into its shell. But a fast predator can bite off the snail's eyes. A conch can fully regrow its eyes in just two weeks!

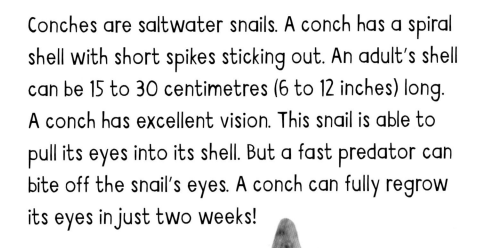

eyes

AFRICAN SPINY MOUSE

The African spiny mouse has skin that can be easily torn. The mouse may lose its skin after a predator attack. This helps the mouse to escape. The African spiny mouse can regenerate its skin immediately after an injury. This is called skin autotomy. It is the first mammal discovered to have this ability.

SEA CUCUMBER

There are more than 1,250 known species of sea cucumbers. They are found near the ocean floor. Sea cucumbers can shoot sticky threads and internal organs at their predators. This confuses the predator so the sea cucumber can get away. Its missing organs regrow quickly. Sea cucumbers live for 5 to 10 years.

FLATWORM

Flatworms are found in places with moist land. They can be as small as 1 millimetre (0.04 inches). But some can grow to 61 centimetres (24 inches)! There are more than 20,000 flatworm species. A flatworm can lose most of its body and regrow from just a small piece. A flatworm is different from most worms. Its tail can regrow a head. And its head can regrow a tail!

GECKO

Geckos use their tails for balance when climbing trees. Some species also use their tails for camouflage. They can blend in with tree bark. Gecko tails have weak points in them. At these weak points, the tail can break off. The fallen tail continues to move. It distracts predators so the gecko has time to escape! One, sometimes two, tails grow back in its place.

:: FUN FACT ::

Geckos are found all around the world, except in Antarctica. They can live in forests, deserts and mountainous areas.

ZEBRAFISH

Zebrafish are freshwater fish originally from India. A zebrafish has two heart chambers. It can regrow its heart muscle. Damaged muscle returns to nearly its original size and shape. A zebrafish can also regrow other body parts. It regenerates bones, blood vessels and nerves in its fins.

WATER BEAR

Tiny water bears live in water in almost every habitat on Earth. A water bear can live in very hot or very cold weather. It can survive in temperatures as low as minus 200 degrees Celsius (minus 328 degrees Fahrenheit). To survive, it goes into a death-like state. It can go without food or water for more than 30 years! When put back into water, a water bear comes back to life – even years later.

:: **FUN FACT** ::
Water bears are also
known as tardigrades.

MOON JELLYFISH

Moon jellyfish are found in warm, open ocean waters. They eat small plankton, fish eggs and other small jellyfish. A moon jellyfish has hair-like parts called cilia. Sometimes a predator takes a bite out of the cilia. The moon jellyfish doesn't regenerate body parts like most jellyfish. Instead, a moon jellyfish rearranges the remaining cilia to fill in the space.

:: FUN FACT ::

A moon jellyfish's colour depends on what it eats.
A pink or purple jellyfish probably eats crustaceans.
An orange jellyfish may be eating brine shrimp.

GLOSSARY

AMPHIBIAN animal that lives in the water when it is young and on land as an adult; some amphibians, such as frogs, can live both in the water and on land as adults

AUTOTOMY ability of some animals to safely shed a damaged or trapped body part

BARK hard covering of a tree

BLOOD VESSEL narrow tube that carries blood through the body

CAMOUFLAGE pattern or colour on an animal's skin that helps it to blend in with the things around it

CARTILAGE strong, flexible material that forms some body parts on humans and animals

CONTRACT tighten and become shorter

DETACH separate one thing from another

LIMB part of the body used in moving or grasping; arms and legs are limbs

MAMMAL warm-blooded animal that breathes air; mammals have hair or fur

NERVE thin fibre that carries messages between the brain and other parts of the body

ORGAN body part that does a certain job

PLANKTON tiny plants and animals that drift in the sea

REGENERATE make new

SPECIES group of animals with similar features

SURVIVE stay alive

BOOKS

Adaptation and Survival (Life Science Stories),
Louise and Richard Spilsbury (Raintree, 2017)

Amazing Animal Shape-Shifters (Animal Scientists),
Leon Gray (Raintree, 2016)

Animal (Eyewitness), DK (DK Children, 2015)

WEBSITES

www.bbc.co.uk/nature/life/Gecko
Learn more about geckos, including an incredible find in the Malaysian
jungle showing a gecko splitting into two species!

**www.dkfindout.com/uk/animals-and-nature/starfish-sea-urchins-and-
sea-cucumbers/**
Find out more about these fascinating underwater survivors.

Comprehension QUESTIONS

1. Which body part can a conch regrow?

2. The African spiny mouse is the first mammal discovered to have the ability to regrow its skin. What is a mammal? Hint: Use the glossary for help!

3. Which animal in this book is your favourite? Why?

::INDEX::